# The Man Who Couldn't Speak

Luke 1:5–25, 57–80; 3:1–36 for children

Written by Jeffrey E. Burkart
Illustrated by Allan Eitzen

**Arch® Books**
Copyright © 1999 Concordia Publishing House
3558 S. Jefferson Avenue, St. Louis, MO 63118-3968
Manufactured in the United States of America

Before our dear Lord Jesus' birth,
A priest named Zechariah
Was with his wife, Elizabeth,
Awaiting the Messiah.

Both Zechariah and his wife
Could not have any children.
They couldn't understand why not.
This problem was bewild'rin'.

Till one day in the temple,
Right beside the incense altar,
An angel of the Lord appeared
And Zechariah faltered.

The angel said, "Don't be afraid!
God knows how you've been praying.
Elizabeth will bear your son!
Now listen to this saying:

"You'll name him John and from his birth
He'll be filled with God's Spirit;
And he'll proclaim, 'God's coming soon!
Let everybody cheer it!'"

Then Zechariah asked,
"How can I know you're being truthful?
I'm wondering just how this can be;
We are no longer youthful!"

"My name is Gabriel,"
The angel answered with conviction.
"And what I have to say to you
Will not bear contradiction!

"God has sent me to proclaim Good News,
But you won't listen!
So this will be a sign to you,
Your voice will now be missin'.

"So from this moment till your baby's born,
You must be quiet.
And you will know God's word is true,
For you cannot deny it."

And when their baby boy was born,
They had a celebration.
Their neighbors and their relatives
Made quite a jubilation!

But much to their surprise that day,
There was an interruption.
Elizabeth spoke up,
And what she said caused a disruption.

"The baby's name is John," she said.
"What can this mean?" they wondered.
They said, "No relative of yours
Has that name—you have blundered!"

Then Zechariah took a tablet
Brought to him for writing.
And as he wrote they held their breath
'Cause it was so exciting!

"His name is John!" the old man wrote,
And with no hesitation,
He sang out loud and praised the Lord
Of every land and nation.

"The light of God will point the way
To peace and to salvation!"
And sure enough, when John grew up,
He made this proclamation:

"The Lord is coming soon!" John said,
"Make straight the crooked highways!
Repent now for the Promised One
Will walk these earthly byways!"

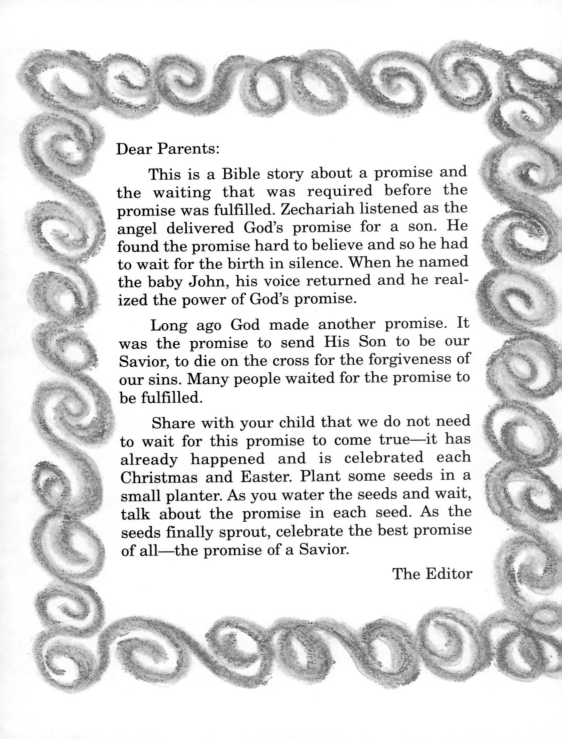

Dear Parents:

This is a Bible story about a promise and the waiting that was required before the promise was fulfilled. Zechariah listened as the angel delivered God's promise for a son. He found the promise hard to believe and so he had to wait for the birth in silence. When he named the baby John, his voice returned and he realized the power of God's promise.

Long ago God made another promise. It was the promise to send His Son to be our Savior, to die on the cross for the forgiveness of our sins. Many people waited for the promise to be fulfilled.

Share with your child that we do not need to wait for this promise to come true—it has already happened and is celebrated each Christmas and Easter. Plant some seeds in a small planter. As you water the seeds and wait, talk about the promise in each seed. As the seeds finally sprout, celebrate the best promise of all—the promise of a Savior.

The Editor